CONTENTS

Author's Preface

The Freedom songs are playing a strong
and vital role in our struggle. They
give the people new courage and a sense
of unity. I think they keep alive a
faith, a radiant hope in the future,
particularly in our most trying hours.

Martin Luther King, Jr.

The songs of the southern sit-in and voter registration movements
of the 1960s are in the direct tradition of protest songs throughout
history. They are uniquely American because they are the direct
descendants of black folk music, which has been singing of "better
days a-comin' " and the "Promised Land" since slavery days.

The old spirituals and work songs were perfectly suited for the
newer, militant lyrics that the largely student-led protesters created
at their lunch-counter sit-ins, public facility picket lines, Freedom
Rides, and, inevitably, in courthouses and jails.

The spiritual *Oh, Freedom*, which was certainly sung in 1860, could
be sung again in 1960 without the need to change any of the words.
And when new words were added to the songs, they often blended in
so easily with what had gone before as to be virtually indistinguish-
able from the traditional material.

Other musical styles also lent themselves admirably to the almost
instant creation so necessary to capture the mood of the moment:
calypso, rock 'n' roll, blues and gospel songs, to name a few. Humor
and satire mingle comfortably with anger and militancy.

Not every song has been preserved for posterity; not every song
could outlive its moment. But the ones that did live, and the ones
that will live, are the true folk songs of their time. What we have in
this collection is just a small sampling of that precious musical legacy
that has come down to us from those young, and not-so-young,
voices that sang of hope, dignity, and freedom a generation ago.

Jerry Silverman

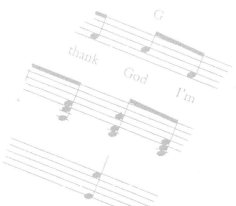

Chorus

D
F#m

Free at last, last, I thank God

D7
Bm

free at last, last,

D G
2. A7 D

I thank God I'm free at last. Oh free at last, last.

On the cover Under threatening skies, protesters make their way on the march from Selma to Montgomery in 1965.

Chelsea House Publishers

Editor-in-Chief   Remmel Nunn
Managing Editor   Karyn Gullen Browne
Copy Chief   Mark Rifkin
Picture Editor   Adrian G. Allen
Art Director   Maria Epes
Assistant Art Director   Howard Brotman
Manufacturing Director   Gerald Levine
Systems Manager   Lindsey Ottman
Production Manager   Joseph Romano
Production Coordinator   Marie Claire Cebrián

Staff for Songs of Protest and Civil Rights

Assistant Editor   Martin Mooney
Picture Researcher   Lisa Kirchner
Book Design   Frank Comito
Cover Design   Howard Brotman

3   5   7   9   8   6   4

Library of Congress Cataloging-in-Publication Data

Songs of protest and civil rights/[compiled by] Jerry Silverman.
   p.   of music.—(Traditional Black music)
   Summary: An illustrated songbook of the black music that was sung during the civil rights protests of the 1960s.
   ISBN 0-7910-1827-X   ISBN 0-7910-1843-1 (pbk.)
   1. Afro-Americans—Music.   2. Afro-Americans—Civil rights—Songs and music.   3. Spirituals (Songs)   [1. Afro-Americans—Civil rights—Songs and music.   2. Civil rights movements—Songs and music.   3. Protest songs.   4. Spirituals (Songs)   5. Songs.]
I. Silverman, Jerry.   II. Series.
M1670.S69   1992   91-32564
                                              CIP   AC M

PICTURE CREDITS
© Peter Arnold, Inc./James H. Karales: cover; Charles Moore/Black Star: p. 55; Schomburg Center for Research in Black Culture, New York Public Library, Astor, Lenox, and Tilden Foundations: p. 17; © Flip Schulke/Black Star: p. 7; © Steve Shapiro/Black Star: p. 25; UPI/Bettmann Archive: pp. 4, 13, 21, 31, 37, 41, 49, 63

The Contribution of Blacks to American Art and Culture

Kenneth B. Clark

Historical and contemporary social inequalities have obscured the major contribution of American blacks to American culture. The historical reality of slavery and the combined racial isolation, segregation, and sustained educational inferiority have had deleterious effects. As related pervasive social problems determine and influence the art that any group can not only experience, but also, ironically, the extent to which they can eventually contribute to the society as a whole, this tenet is even more visible when assessing the contributions made by African Americans.

All aspects of the arts have been pursued by black Americans, but music provides a special insight into the persistent and inescapable social forces to which black Americans have been subjected. One can speculate that in their preslavery patterns of life in Africa, blacks used rhythm, melody, and lyrics to hold on to reality, hope, and the acceptance of life. Later, in America, music helped blacks endure the cruelties of slavery. Spirituals and gospel music provided a medium for both communion and communication. As the black experience in America became more complex, so too did black music, which has grown and ramified, dramatically affecting the development of American music in general. The result is that today, more than ever before, black music provides a powerful lens through which we may view the history of black Americans in a new and revealing way.

Steel bars may have been able to confine the bodies of these demonstrators in a Birmingham, Alabama, jail in 1963, but their spirit—and the spirit of the entire civil rights movement—would not be dampened by any jail cell.

In February 1962, some eighty students were expelled from Albany State College in Georgia. They had been participating in demonstrations at the bus and train stations and at the city courthouse. Many of the students wound up in jail, where they improvised and harmonized on gospel, spiritual, rock 'n' roll, and popular songs with new freedom lyrics. This is one of their songs.

FREEDOM IN THE AIR

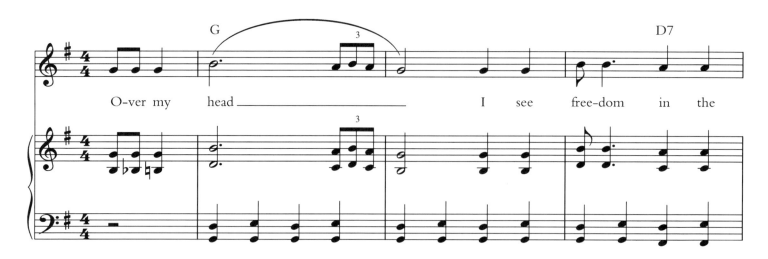

O-ver my head _____ I see free-dom in the

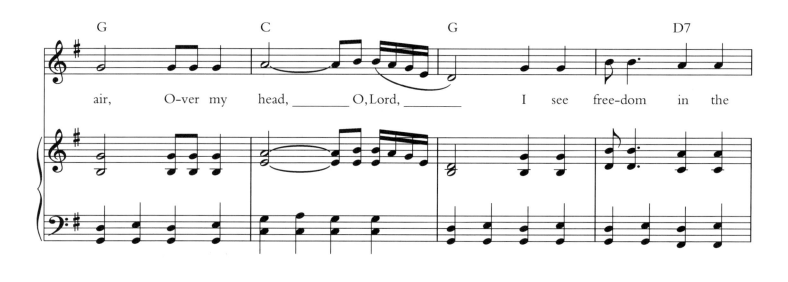

air, O-ver my head, _____ O, Lord, _____ I see free-dom in the

air, O-ver my head _____ I see free - dom in the

Over my head I see justice in the air,
Over my head, O, Lord, I see justice in the air,
Over my head I see justice in the air,
There must be a God somewhere.

Over my head I see victory in the air . . .

Freedom—and hope—is in the air at the march on Washington in 1963, when more than 250,000 people—black and white—rallied to support the civil rights bill, which was being voted on in Congress.

As three hundred foot-weary but light-souled people stopped for a rest, sitting in the grass along Alabama's Route 80, I tried to write down the melodies of some of the dozens of new songs I had heard. A woman watched me and laughed, "Don't you know you can't write down freedom songs?" —which I know has been said by everyone who has tried to capture Negro folk music with European musical notation. Furthermore, when I asked, "Can you give me the words to? `Oh, Wallace'?" ★ they kept answering, "Man, there are no words, you just make them up."

—Pete Seeger, folksinger, March 24, 1965

OH, WALLACE

Oh, __ Wal-lace! You nev-er can jail us all _____

_____ Oh, __ Wal-lace! Seg - re - ga - tion's bound to fall, __

Da dat __ do dat dat, da da da da da da dat, Da dat __ da da dat.

* George A. Wallace—Governor of Alabama

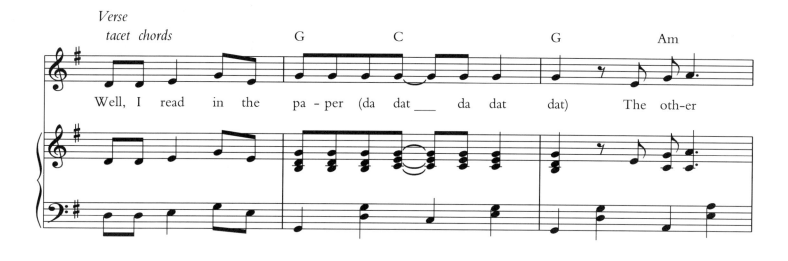

Well, I read in the pa-per (da dat ___ da dat dat) The oth-er

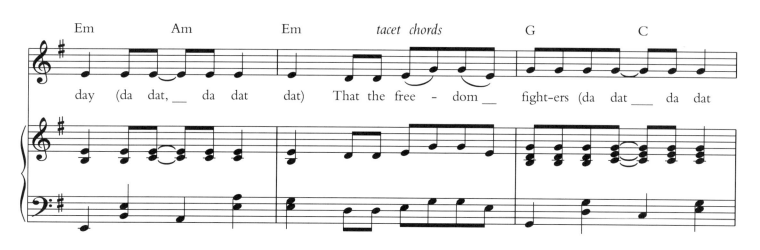

day (da dat, ___ da dat dat) That the free - dom ___ fight-ers (da dat ___ da dat

dat) Are on their way. (Da dat ___ da dat dat) Oh, _____

They're coming by bus (da dat da dat dat)
And airplane too (da dat da dat dat)
They'll even walk (da dat da dat dat)
If you ask them to. (da dat da dat dat)

I don't want no mess . . .
I don't want no jive . . .
And I want my freedom . . .
In 'sixty-five . . .

Tell Al Lingo
And Jim Clark too
We want our freedom
And we want it now.

The ocean is deep . . .
The river is wide . . .
I'll find my freedom . . .
On the other side . . .

Don't worry about . . .
Going to jail . . .
'Cause Martin Luther King . . .
Will go your bail . . .

He'll get you out . . .
Right on time . . .
Put you back . . .
On the picket line . . .

For years after the victory celebrated in *Hallelujah! I'm A-Travelin'*, where black people were allowed to sit on local buses in the South was still a burning issue. As old and new battles continued to be fought during the 1960s, segregated bus seating retained its symbolic value, with other campaigns "zipped" in.

IF YOU MISS ME FROM THE BACK OF THE BUS

If you miss __ me from the back of the bus, __ And you can't find __ me no-

where, come on up __ to the front of the bus, __

I'll be rid - ing up there, I'll be rid - ing up there,

If you miss me from the front of the bus,
And you can't find me nowhere,
Come on up to the driver's seat,
I'll be drivin' up there.
    I'll be drivin' up there,
    I'll be drivin' up there,
Come on up to the driver's seat,
    I'll be drivin' up there.

If you miss me from Jackson State . . .
Come on over to Ole Miss,
I'll be studyin' over there . . .

If you miss me from knockin' on doors . . .
Come on down to the registrar's room,
I'll be the registrar there . . .

If you miss me from the cotton field . . .
Come on down to the courthouse,
I'll be votin' right there . . .

If you miss me from the picket line . . .
Come on down to the jail house,
I'll be roomin' down there . . .

If you miss me from the Mississippi River . . .
Come on down to the city pool,
I'll be swimming in there . . .

When protesting students were arrested and thrown into jails across the South for demonstrating and protesting, they made the jail houses ring with song. In this song, the leader asks the question and the group responds. This traditional, time-honored pattern is perfect for expressing feelings and getting a message across.

CERTAINLY, LORD

Additional verses

Well, did they give you thirty days? . . .

Well, did you serve your time? . . .

Well, will you go back again? . . .

Well, will you fight for freedom? . . .

Well, will you tell it to the world? . . .

Well, will you tell it to the judge? . . .

The road to equality often has many detours. These protesters, jailed in East St. Louis, Illinois, in 1963, know there will be many more.

The Promised Land of the Bible took on a very special significance for slaves before the Civil War. After the emancipation, the Promised Land still remained a goal yet to be fully achieved. It is no wonder that this powerful image still retained its force into the 1960s—and to this very day.

COME AND GO WITH ME TO THAT LAND

land, Come and go with me to that land __ where I'm bound. _____

There'll be no Jim Crow in that land,
There'll be no Jim Crow in that land,
There'll be no Jim Crow in that land,
 Where I'm bound.
There'll be no Jim Crow in that land,
There'll be no Jim Crow in that land,
There'll be no Jim Crow in that land,
 Where I'm bound.

No burning churches in that land . . .

There'll be singing in that land . . .

There'll be freedom in that land . . .

Peace and plenty in that land . . .

It may be hard to imagine how "sitting at the welcome table" or "walking the streets of glory" or "telling God how you treat me" can be tied in with something as seemingly commonplace as "sitting at Woolworth's lunch counter"—but the fact is that Woolworth's lunch counters (among many others) used to be simply off limits to black people in the South. The strength and the beauty of this song lies in the joining of the spiritual with the earthly.

I'M GONNA SIT AT THE WELCOME TABLE

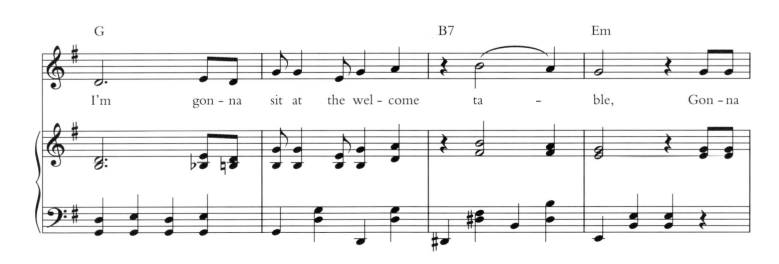

sit at the wel-come ta-ble one of these days. _____

I'm gonna walk the streets of glory,
I'm gonna walk the streets of glory
    One of these days, hallelujah.
I'm gonna walk the streets of glory,
I'm gonna walk the streets of glory.
    One of these days.

I'm gonna tell God how you treat me . . .

I'm gonna get my civil rights . . .

I'm gonna sit at Woolworth's lunch counter . . .

Segregation was fought on buses, in universities, and at lunch counters, including this protest against Woolworth's in the early 1960s.

This song, composed by a southern black farmer, celebrates the 1946 Supreme Court ruling outlawing segregated seating on interstate bus travel. When the song was first published in the September 1946 issue of *People's Songs,* the following comment was added: "For obvious reasons we can't mention the name or whereabouts of the author."

HALLELUJAH! I'M A-TRAVELIN'

Stand up and re - joice! A ___ great day is here! We're ___

fight - ing Jim Crow and the vic - to - ry's near! Hal - le -

lu - jah, I'm a-trav - el - in', Hal - le - lu - jah, ain't it fine. Hal - le -

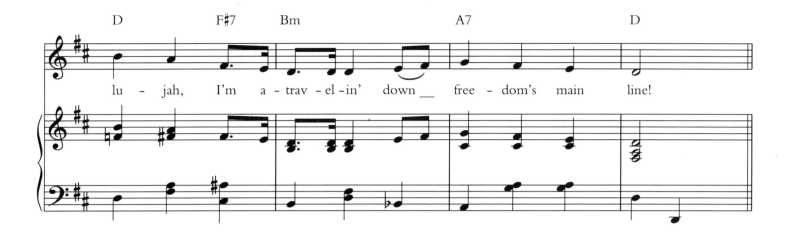

lu - jah, I'm a - trav - el -in' down __ free - dom's main line!

Original 1946 verses

I read in the news the Supreme Court has said,
"Listen here, Mister Jim Crow, it's time you was dead." *Chorus*

The judges declared in Washington town,
"You white folks must take that old Jim Crow sign down." *Chorus*

I'm paying my fare on the Greyhound Bus line,
I'm riding the front seat to Nashville this time. *Chorus*

Columbia's the gem of the ocean, they say,
We're fighting Jim Crow in Columbia today. *Chorus*

I hate Jim Crow and Jim Crow hates me,
And that's why I'm fighting for my liberty. *Chorus*

Verses from the 1960s

In 1954 our Supreme Court said,
"Look a-here Mr. Jim Crow, it's time you were dead." *Chorus*

I'm paying my fare on the Greyhound Bus line,
I'm riding the front seat to Montgomery this time. *Chorus*

In Nashville, Tennessee, I can order a coke,
And the waitress at Woolworth's knows it's no joke. *Chorus*

In old Fayette County, set off and remote,
The polls are now open for Negroes to vote. *Chorus*

I walked in Montgomery, I sat in Tennessee,
And now I'm riding for equality. *Chorus*

I'm travelin' to Mississippi on the Greyhound Bus line,
Hallelujah, I'm ridin' the front seat this time. *Chorus*

Of West Indian extraction, Al Wood grew up in New York City. His musical tradition is calypso, and it is in this rhythmic style that he wrote this song in 1952.

MY PEOPLE WILL RISE

By Albert Wood

Calypso

We're going to rise, My peo-ple will rise, __ I know some day my

peo-ple will rise, __ So smile, Miss No-ra and dry your eyes

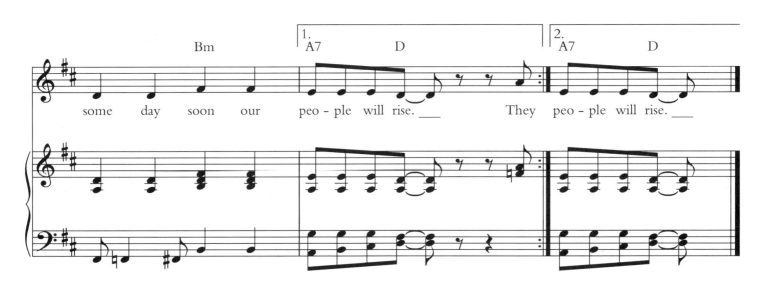

some day soon our peo-ple will rise. ___ They peo-ple will rise. ___

The verses are sung to the entire eight-measure melody.
The chorus is sung to the last four measures.

They call us savage
And they make us slave,
'Cause in their minds
They're the ones depraved,
The heel is used
To try and grind us down,
But some day soon
There'll be a turnaround. *Chorus*

They say that women are weak
And you know that's wrong,
Because with our women
We'll be twice as strong,
The whip will change
To the other hand,
With a surge of power
We're bound to free the land. *Chorus*

The big money man
Getting richer too,
But the sweat is coming
From me and you;
Let's all unite
And make a stand,
And share in the profit
Of our grand, rich land. *Chorus*

When I speak of people
I mean us all,
The fat, the thin,
The short and the tall,
No mention must be made
Of race or creed,
'Cause a thing like that
A product of greed. *Chorus*

Men and women join together in a demonstration in Cicero, Illinois, in 1966.

This simple yet powerfully moving hymn was the theme song of the civil right movement of the 1960s. It is rooted in an old black church song, *I'll Overcome Some Day*. In the 1940s the old song was adapted by members of the Food and Tobacco Workers Union, and it was first sung in Charleston, South Carolina. It was during that period that the song found its way to the Highlander Folk School in Tennessee. Zilphia Horton, the school's director, introduced it to union gatherings all across the South. On one of Zilphia's trips to New York, Pete Seeger heard her singing and during the next few years helped spread it all over the country. Some of the words were changed to fit new situations, particularly the struggle for civil rights. It has been sung at great mass rallies by thousands of voices and has echoed around the world in many languages.

WE SHALL OVERCOME

22

We are not afraid,
We are not afraid,
We are not afraid today.
Oh, deep in my heart, I do believe,
We shall overcome some day.

We are not alone . . . (today) . . .

The truth will make us free . . . (some day) . . .

We'll walk hand in hand . . . (today) . . .

The Lord will see us through . . . (today) . . .

Repeat first verse

WE SHALL OVERCOME
By Zilphia Horton, Frank Hamilton, Guy Carawan, & Pete Seeger. TRO—Copyright 1960
(renewed) and 1963 (renewed) Ludlow Music, Inc., New York, NY. Used by permission.
Royalties derived from this composition are being contributed to the Freedom Movement
under the trusteeship of the writers.

The Nashville jails echoed with this adaptation of the spiritual "Amen." When students who had been arrested at sit-ins were brought to trial, a crowd of 2,500 people gathered around the courthouse. In the traditional manner, the leader lined out the opening phrases and the crowd responded with: "Freedom!"

EVERYBODY SING FREEDOM

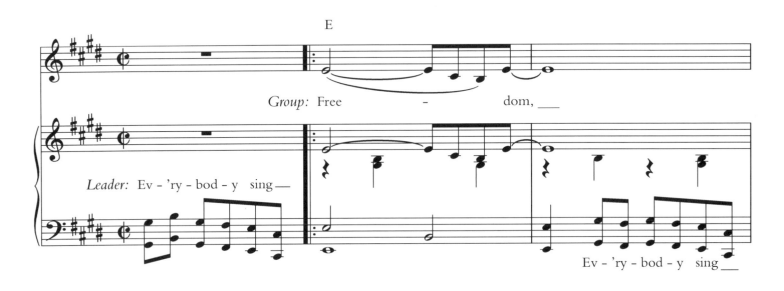

Leader

Fight for freedom . . .
Gain the victory . . .
In the jail house . . .
In the cotton fields . . .
In Mississippi . . .
All across the South . . .
All across the country . . .

In the fight for freedom we must all stand together, for there is no movement without unity.

Joshua fought the battle of Jericho, Jericho, Jericho,
Joshua fought the battle of Jericho,
And the walls came tumbling down!

From biblical times, when Joshua's trumpets caused the walls of Jericho to come tumbling down, the power of music and song has been recognized as a vital ingredient in any popular struggle. The leaders of the Student Nonviolent Coordinating Committee recognized the value of songs, and the students themselves sang songs, old and new, at their mass meetings and at their mass arrests.

SING TILL THE POWER OF THE LORD COMES DOWN

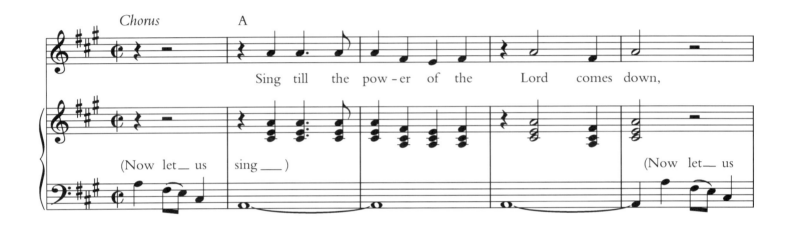

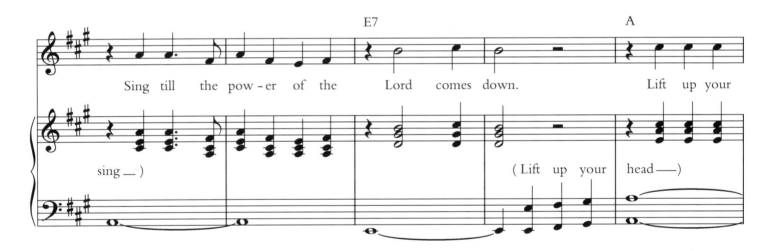

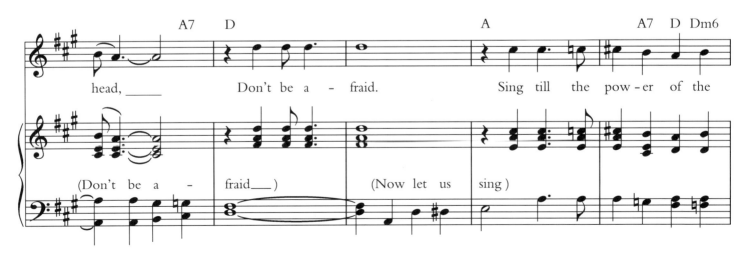

In the summer of 1960, a workshop for singers, song leaders, and songwriters was held at the Highlander Folk School in Mounteagle, Tennessee. The people who attended the workshop were active in the integration movement in the South and included gospel groups from Montgomery and Birmingham, in Alabama. These groups introduced this old spiritual to the participants at the workshop. Everybody present immediately realized the song's relevance to the struggle for equal rights that was under way.

WE ARE SOLDIERS IN THE ARMY

We are sol-diers in the ar - my, We've got to fight, _____ Al -

though we have _ to cry. We've got to hold, _____ hold _____ up the free-dom ban-ner, Take it

home, _ We got to hold it up un-til we die. __ My moth-er _____ was a

sol-dier, She had her hand on the gos - pel plow, ___ But one

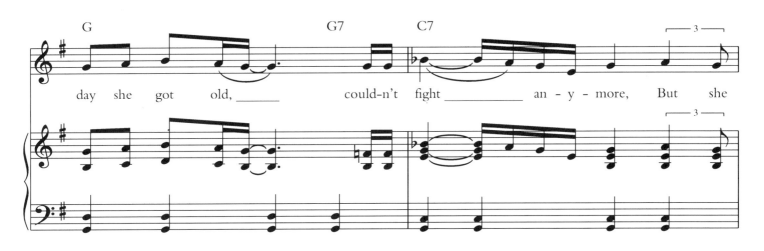

day she got old, ___ could-n't fight ___ an - y - more, But she

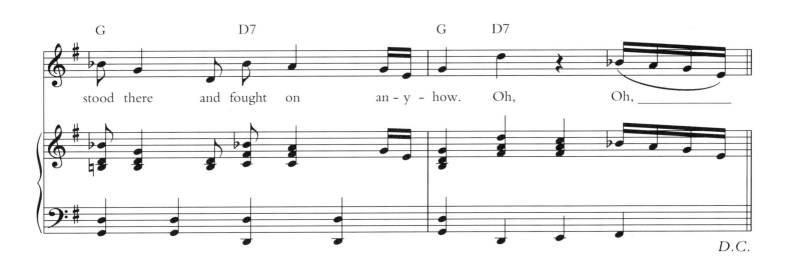

stood there and fought on an - y - how. Oh, Oh, ___

D.C.

I'm glad I am a soldier
I've got my hand on the gospel plow
But one day I'll get old, I can't fight anymore
I'll just stand here and fight on anyhow. *Chorus*

I know I've been converted,
And of this I am not ashamed.
I was standing right there at the station,
When the holy ghost signed my name. *Chorus*

This timeless ballad can be sung whenever and wherever people are struggling for freedom and human dignity.

CARRY IT ON

By Gil Turner

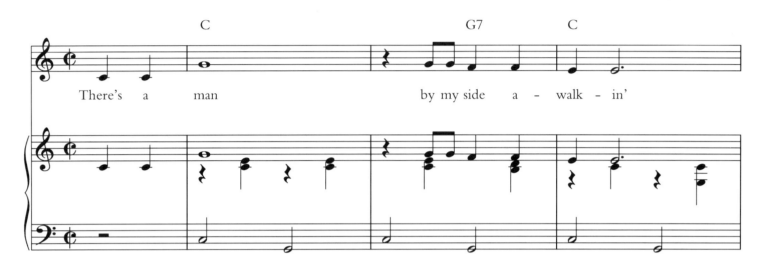

There's a man by my side a - walk - in'

There's a voice in - side me a - talk - in'

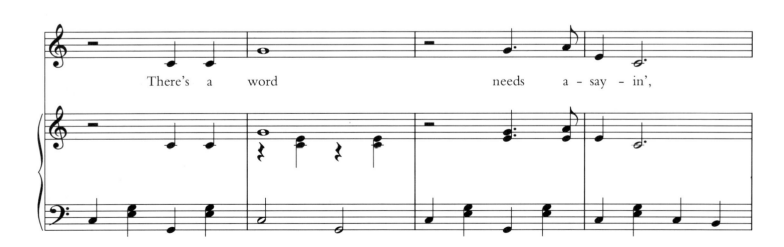

There's a word needs a - say - in',

Car-ry it on, _____ car-ry it on, _____

Car-ry it on, _____ car - ry it on. _____

They will tell their lyin' stories
Send their dogs to bite our bodies
They will lock us in prison,
Carry it on, carry it on,
Carry it on, carry it on.

All their lies be soon forgotten
All their dogs will lie there rottin'
All their prison walls will crumble,
Carry it on, carry it on,
Carry it on, carry it on.

If you can't go on any longer
Take the hand held by your brother
Every victory gonna bring another,
Carry it on, carry it on,
Carry it on, carry it on.

The march on Washington in 1963 lit a torch that people today still must carry.

In Baton Rouge, Louisiana, Bob Zellner, Student Nonviolent Coordinating Committee field secretary, is arrested, jailed, and indicted for "criminal anarchy." What does he do when he is released? He adapts an old song to fit a new situation.

BEEN DOWN INTO THE SOUTH

I have-n't been to Heav-en, but I think I'm right, _____ Been down in-

to the South. __ There's folks up there both black and white, _____ Been down in-

to the South. _ Hal - le - lu - jah Free-dom, Hal - le -

lu – jah Free-dom,   Hal – le – lu – jah Free-dom, _____

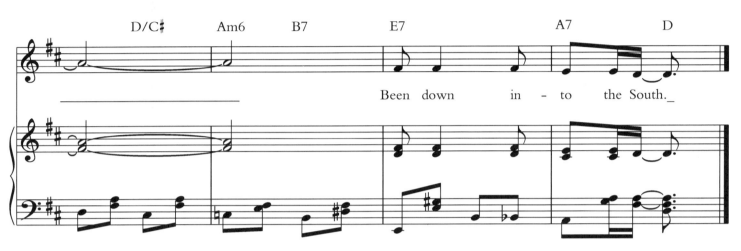

_____   Been down in – to the South.

I want to go to heaven but I want to go right,
Been down into the South.
I don't want to go without my civil rights,
Been down into the South. *Chorus*

Segregation is chilly and cold . . .
Chills my body but not my soul . . . *Chorus*

Freedom sounds so mighty sweet . . .
Soon one day we're gonna meet . . . *Chorus*

I been knockin' on doors and spreadin' the news . . .
And gettin' big holes in the bottom of my shoes . . . *Chorus*

Yes I've got big holes in the bottom of my shoes . . .
But this is one battle we can't lose . . . *Chorus*

If you don't think I've been through Hell . . .
Just follow me down to the Parchman jail . . . *Chorus*

You can talk about me just as much as you please,
Well the more you talk I'm gonna bend my knees . . . *Chorus*

The only thing that we did wrong . . .
Stayed in the wilderness a day too long . . . *Chorus*

The only thing that we did right . . .
Was the day we started to fight . . . *Chorus*

We are fighting both black and white . . .
Fighting for our civil rights . . . *Chorus*

This song was first published in *Sing Out* in September 1952. The Negro soldier in verse two is a veteran of World War II.

NOW, RIGHT NOW!

I met a Ne-gro moth-er, Her head was bent and low, She said why do the po-lice treat my peo-ple so? They beat us and they starve us, while jus-tice pass-es by, That's why I'll fight for free-dom and hold my head up __ high. Now, right __

now, Now right now, __ Now's the time for free - dom,

Now, right now. Do __ right _ now, and fight right

now, __ Fight the fight for free - dom, Now, right _ now.

I met a Negro soldier, coming from the war,
I asked that Negro soldier what he'd been fighting for.
Said that Negro soldier, "Me, I took a vow—
I was fighting for my freedom, and I want it now, right now!" *Chorus*

I've had my share of troubles, I've had my share and more,
But I added up my troubles and now I know the score;
Our wrongs shall all be righted—our strength shall show us how,
With blacks and whites united—I mean now, right now! *Chorus*

We were crammed into a narrow hallway to await booking and I studied the faces around me. . . . We sang a good part of our eight-hour confinement that first time. The city policemen seemed to enjoy the singing. . . . We were a change from the Saturday night drunk who rarely sang.

—Candie Anderson, a white exchange student at Fisk University, February 1960, on the sit-ins that had started in Nashville and landed her and many of her black classmates in a segregated cell in the Nashville City Jail.

HOW DID YOU FEEL

Oh, tell me, how did you feel ___ when you come out the wil – der – ness,

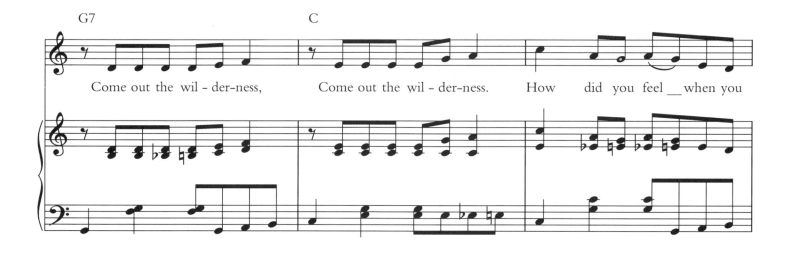

Come out the wil – der – ness, Come out the wil – der – ness. How did you feel ___ when you

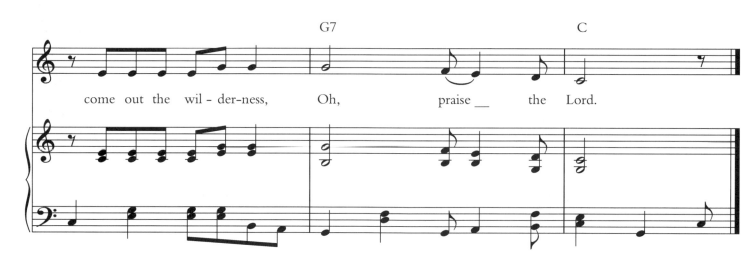

come out the wil – der – ness, Oh, praise ___ the Lord.

Oh, did you feel like fighting when you
    Come out the wilderness,
    Come out the wilderness,
    Come out the wilderness.
Oh, did you feel like fighting when you
    Come out the wilderness,
Oh, praise the Lord.

Oh, will you fight for freedom . . .

Oh, will you walk the line . . .

Oh, will you carry a sign . . .

Oh, will you go to jail . . .

Civil disobedience was a major weapon in the civil rights movement of the 1960s.
These protesters are arrested at a demonstration in Elizabeth, New Jersey, in 1963.

The original chorus of this song went, "Keep your hand on the plow, hold on." In 1956, Alice Wine of Johns Island, South Carolina, who was one of the first proud products of voter education schools, had a different vision and changed the words.

KEEP YOUR EYES ON THE PRIZE

Paul and Si - las bound in jail, ___ Had no mon-ey for to go their bail, ___

Chorus

___ Keep your eyes on ___ the prize, ___ hold ___ on, hold

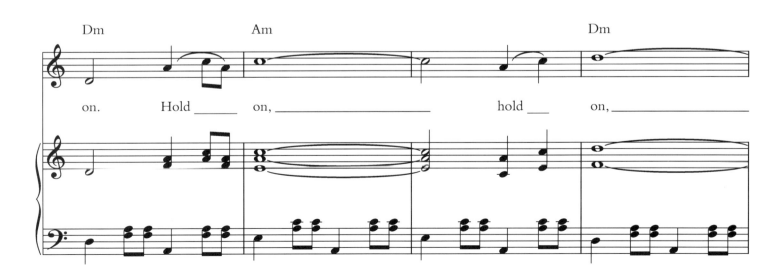

on. Hold _____ on, _____ hold ___ on, _____

Keep your eyes on the prize, Hold on, hold on.

Paul and Silas begin to shout,
The jail door opened and they walked on out. *Chorus*

Freedom's name is mighty sweet,
Soon one day we're gonna meet. *Chorus*

Got my hand on the Gospel plow,
I wouldn't take nothing for my journey now. *Chorus*

The only chain that a man can stand,
Is that chain of hand in hand. *Chorus*

The only thing we did wrong,
Stayed in the wilderness a day too long. *Chorus*

But the one thing we did right,
Was the day we started to fight. *Chorus*

We're gonna board that big Greyhound,
Carryin' love from town to town. *Chorus*

We're gonna ride for civil rights,
We're gonna ride both black and white. *Chorus*

We've met jail and violence too,
But God's love has seen us through. *Chorus*

Haven't been to Heaven but I've been told,
Streets up there are paved with gold. *Chorus*

This song had a long and honorable history as a union picket-line song years before the civil rights movement took it on. Before that, it was a gospel hymn.

WE SHALL NOT BE MOVED

We shall not, we shall not be moved, __

We shall not, we shall not be moved. Just like a

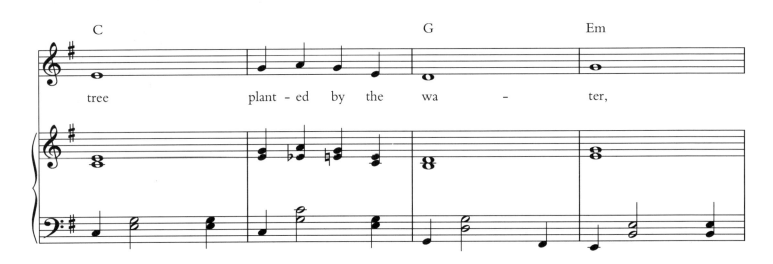

tree plant - ed by the wa - ter,

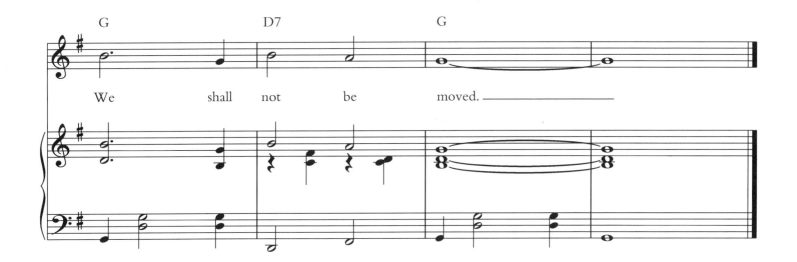

We shall not be moved.

We're fighting for our freedom,
  We shall not be moved,
We're fighting for our freedom,
  We shall not be moved,
Just like a tree planted by the water,
  We shall not be moved. *Chorus*

We're black and white together . . .

We'll stand and fight together . . .

The government is behind us . . .

Our parks are integrating . . .

We're sunning on the beaches . . .

We're marching on to victory . . .

"I have a dream," said Dr. Martin Luther King, Jr., at the march on Washington in 1963. These words sparked one of the biggest social upheavals—the civil rights movement—that the United States has ever seen.

On August 28, 1963, more than a quarter of a million people—from all over America—assembled in Washington, D.C., on the grassy slope of the Washington Monument and then walked about a mile to the Lincoln Memorial. They had one thing in mind, and although many speakers and singers said it differently, it remained for Martin Luther King, Jr., to say it once and for all for everybody. This is how he concluded his famous "I Have a Dream" speech:

> And when we allow freedom to ring, when we let it ring from every village and every hamlet, from every state and every city, we will be able to speed up that day when all of God's children, black men and white men, Jews and Gentiles, Protestants and Catholics, will be able to join hands and sing in the words of that old Negro spiritual, "Free at last! Free at last! Thank God almighty, we are free at last!"

FREE AT LAST

Fine

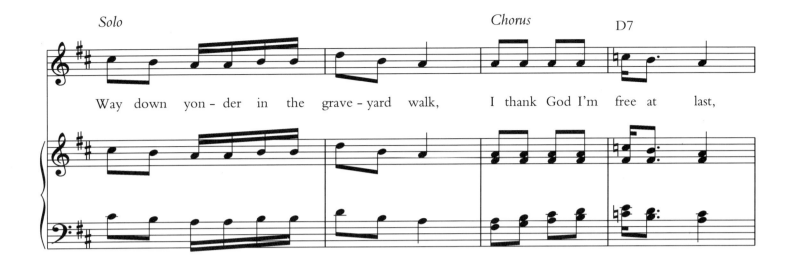

Way down yon-der in the grave-yard walk, I thank God I'm free at last,

Me and my Je-sus gon-na meet and talk,___ I thank God I'm free at last. Oh,

On my knees when the light passed by,
I thank God I'm free at last,
Thought my soul would rise and fly,
I thank God I'm free at last. *Chorus*

Some of these mornings, bright and fair,
I thank God I'm free at last,
Gonna meet my Jesus in the middle of the air,
I thank God I'm free at last. *Chorus*

You mought be rich as cream,
And drive you a coach and four-horse team;
But you can't keep the world from moving around,
And Nat Turner from the gaining ground.

On Sunday, August 21, 1831, Nat Turner gathered a half-dozen fellow slaves and set out from his master's plantation in Southampton County, Virgina, to free the South from slavery. It was a bloody uprising that was doomed to failure from the beginning. By the time Turner was captured and executed nine days later, about 150 people—black and white—had been killed. Slave owners were never again to be free of the fear of similar uprisings.

OH, FREEDOM

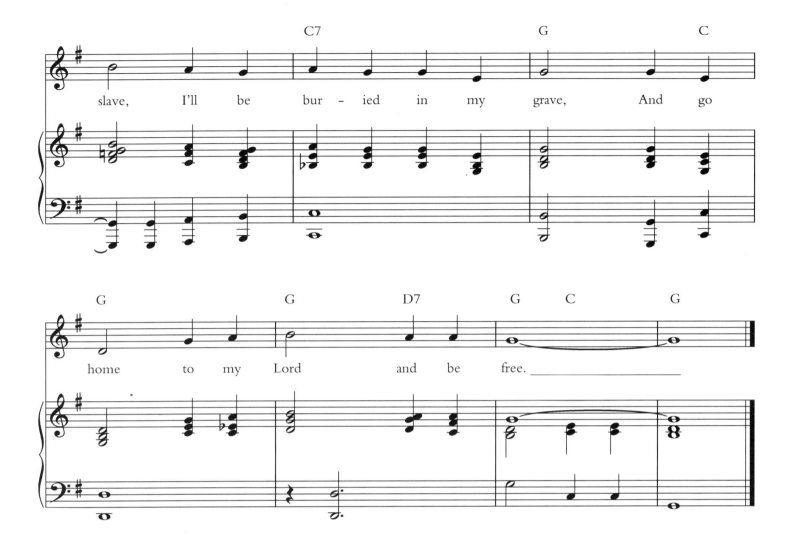

Original Verses

No more moaning, no more moaning,
No more moaning over me.
And before I'll be a slave,
I'll be buried in my grave,
And go home to my Lord and be free.

No more weeping . . .

There'll be singing . . .

Verses from the 1960s

No more shooting . . .

No burning churches . . .

No more jail house . . .

No more Jim Crow . . .

In 1957, Bill McAdoo was a student at the University of Michigan. When the Montgomery Bus Boycott ended in victory, he was moved to write this song. He set his words to a traditional twelve-bar blues form.

WALK ON, ALABAMA

By Bill McAdoo

You get a fine for look - ing a fine for talk - ing, but the

best damn fine is that fine for walk - ing. Walk on, Al - a - bam-a,

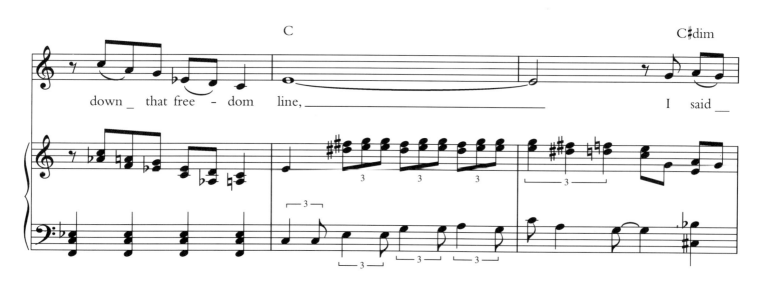

down __ that free - dom line, _____ I said __

walk on, Al - a - bam-a, you're a friend of mine.

Final Ending

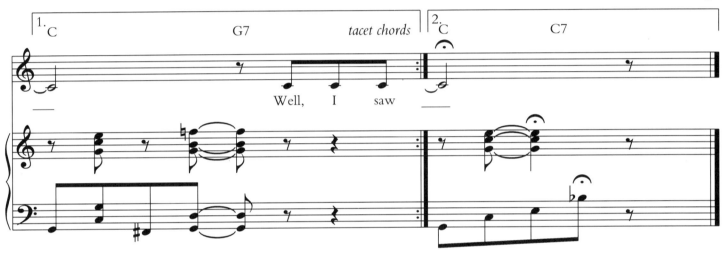

Well, I saw

I saw Reverend King at the head of the line,
I said, "Hey there Reverend, where're we goin?" He said, *Chorus*

Those jail house walls are mighty and tall,
When the people shout those walls gonna fall. *Chorus*

If we don't ride those buses don't roll,
Gonna quit payin' money to that old Jim Crow. *Chorus*

Come on brother, join our line,
Cause I'm sick and tired of those Jim Crow signs. *Chorus*

I'm an old man and I'm ninety-four,
Gonna walk to heaven, won't ride no more. *Chorus*

Paid full fare on that bus line,
Gonna ride the front seat all the time. *Chorus*

I was expelled from my high school [in Lee County] for speaking up for better facilities and more civil rights. . . . When the administration refused to let me back in, the students boycotted the school for over three months. . . . During this time I tried to register [to vote]. . . . But the county officials refused to let me. . . . Soon our home was fired into . . . then the Shady Grove Baptist Church was burned. . . .

—Charles Wingfield, who wrote this song with his friend Charles Neblett, after Neblett's experiences in the Charleston, Mississippi, jail.

FIGHTING FOR MY RIGHTS

You know I'm tired of seg - re-ga-tion and I want my e - qual rights. _ Seg - re - ga - tion did me wrong, _ made me leave my hap - py home, _ That's why I'm fight - ing for my rights, _____ fight - ing for my rights, You know I'm

fight - ing for my rights, __ You know I'm fight - ing for my rights. __

My mother, yeah, she told me
On her dying bed,
Son, if you don't get your freedom,
You know I'd rather see you dead. *Chorus*

Well my father, yes, he told me
A long, long time ago,
Son, if you don't fight for freedom,
You'll be a slave forever more. *Chorus*

Well-a I want my freedom,
And I want it now.
And no matter what happens,
I'm gonna fight on anyhow. *Chorus*

Well my cell it had two windows,
But the sun could never come through,
And I left so sad and lonely,
You know I didn't know what to do. *Chorus*

Well an old lady told me,
And she was very brave,
She said before she'll be a slave,
She'd be buried in her grave. *Chorus*

The aftermath of an ugly attack on a bus carrying Congress of Racial Equality (CORE)
Freedom Riders in Anniston, Alabama, in 1961.

I Woke Up This Morning with My Mind on Jesus is the name of an old gospel song. Reverend Osby of Aurora, Illinois, rewrote the words while in jail in Hinds County, Mississippi, during the Freedom Rides in 1961. It was soon being sung in nearby McComb, where one of the earliest black voter registration campaigns had begun. From there it spread throughout the South—wherever the struggle for equal rights was being carried on.

WOKE UP THIS MORNING WITH MY MIND ON FREEDOM

Woke up this morn - ing with my mind
Walk - in' and talk - in' with my mind
Ain't ___ no harm ___ to keep your mind
Ev - er - y - bod - y's got his mind

stayed _____ on

free - dom. ___

Woke up this morn - ing with my mind _____
Walk - in' and talk - in' with my mind _____
Ain't __ no harm _ to keep your mind _____
Ev - er - y - bod - y's got his mind _____

stayed _____ on

Woke up this morn – ing with my mind
Walk –in' and talk – in' with my mind
Ain't __ no harm _ to keep your mind
Ev – er – y – bod – y's got his mind

free - dom, __   stayed _____ on

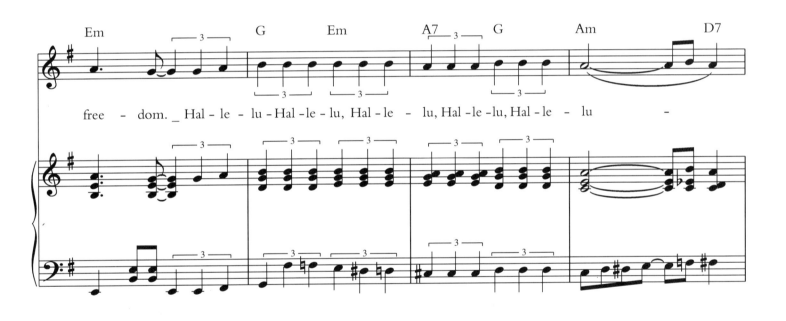

free - dom. _ Hal – le – lu –Hal –le –lu, Hal –le – lu, Hal –le –lu, Hal –le – lu -

jah.   Walk,   walk, _   walk,   walk, _   walk,   walk _ with my

mind on free - dom, __ walk, walk, __ walk, walk, __

walk, walk __ with my mind on free - dom. Ah, _____

ah, _____ walk, walk, __ walk, walk. __

In its original form, this song is known as *Kumbaya*. It is widely sung in schools and is often thought of as a childrens' song.

Come by Here

Come by here, my Lord, come by here. Come by here, my Lord, come by

here. come by here, my Lord, come by here, O Lord, ___ come by here.

Churches burning, Lord, come by here,
Churches burning, Lord, come by here,
Churches burning, Lord, come by here,
 Oh, Lord, come by here.

Someone's weeping, Lord, come by here,
Someone's weeping, Lord, come by here,
Someone's weeping, Lord, come by here,
 Oh, Lord, come by here.

Someone's shooting, Lord, come by here,
Someone's shooting, Lord, come by here,
Someone's shooting, Lord, come by here,
 Oh, Lord, come by here.

We want justice, Lord, come by here,
We want justice, Lord, come by here,
We want justice, Lord, come by here,
 Oh, Lord, come by here.

We want freedom, Lord, come by here,
We want freedom, Lord, come by here,
We want freedom, Lord, come by here,
 Oh, Lord, come by here.

A recurrent theme in many of the civil rights songs is joy—joy in fighting the good fight. This spirit comes directly from the church, with its dual message of salvation and redemption.

I'M SO GLAD

I'm so glad I'm fight-ing to be free,

I'm so glad I'm fight-ing to be free,

I'm so glad I'm fight-ing to be free, sing-ing

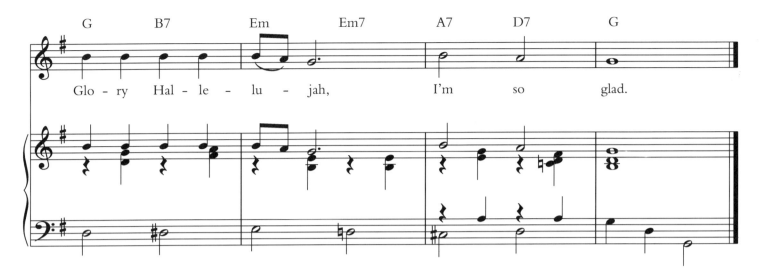

Glo - ry Hal - le - lu - jah, I'm so glad.

I'm so glad jail can't stop us now, (3)
Singing Glory Hallelujah, I'm so glad.

I'm so glad we shall overcome, (3)
Singing Glory Hallelujah, I'm so glad.

I'm so glad our faith will see us through (3)
Singing Glory Hallelujah, I'm so glad.

Mississippi's time has come, (3)
Singing Glory Hallelujah, I'm so glad.

I'm so glad I'm riding to be free (3)
Singing Glory Hallelujah, I'm so glad.

The civil rights movement was brought into America's consciousness during the Birmingham protests in 1963.
Even though often harrassed and attacked by racist police forces, these marchers remained undaunted.

Albany, Georgia, during the summer of 1962 was the scene of mass demonstrations and mass arrests. One night, the Reverend Ralph Abernathy taught this song to a mass meeting of the black community at the Mount Zion Baptist Church. It caught on immediately and became widely used in the demonstrations. When in a later demonstration singing students were being carried into paddy wagons by the police, CBS cameras captured the scene and the song and televised it to the entire nation.

AIN'T GONNA LET NOBODY TURN ME 'ROUND

Ain't gon - na let ___ no - bod - y, Lor - dy, turn me 'round, turn me 'round, turn me 'round, Ain't gon - na let ___ no - bod - y, Lord - y, turn me 'round, I'm gon - na keep on a - walk - in', Lord,

keep on a - talk - in', Lord, march - ing up to free - dom land.____

Ain't gonna let segregation turn me 'round,
  Turn me 'round, turn me 'round,
Ain't gonna let segregation turn me 'round,
  I'm gonna keep on a-walkin',
Keep on a-talkin',
Marching up to freedom land.

Ain't gonna let no jail house turn me 'round . . .

Ain't gonna let no police dogs turn me 'round . . .

Ain't gonna let no sherrif deputies turn me 'round . . .

One of the great strengths of the singing civil rights movement was the students' ability to take a traditional song and adapt it by adding the name of a particular person who would be known to one and all. In this case, arch-segregationist Governor Ross Barnett of Mississippi (1960-64) was so "honored."

Songs are easy. A lot we make up as we go, mostly in jail. We were sitting around a drugstore today and I made up a song in rock 'n' roll style. But the movement is constantly on people's minds. First they sing rock 'n' roll and then they go into these freedom songs.

—Cordell Reagon, student leader

GET ON BOARD, LITTLE CHILDREN

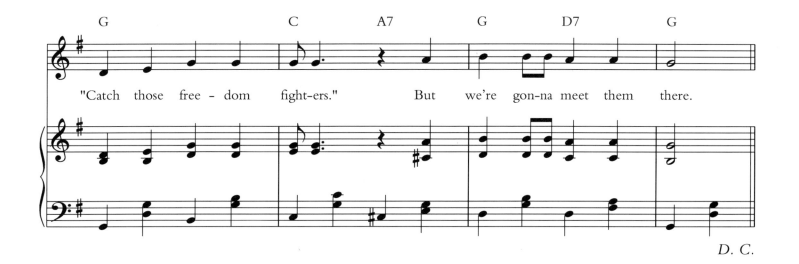

"Catch those free-dom fight-ers." But we're gon-na meet them there.

D. C.

As fighters we're not running,
For we are here to stay.
Forget about Ross Barnett
The Lord will make a way. *Chorus*

As fighters we all realize
That we may go to jail.
But if you fight for freedom,
There's no such thing as bail. *Chorus*

Can't you see that mob a-comin',
Comin' 'round the bend.
If you fight for freedom,
They'll try to do you in. *Chorus*

As fighters we go hungry,
Sometimes don't sleep or eat.
We're fighting for our freedom
And someday we'll be free. *Chorus*

During the cotton harvest of 1936, a group of white thugs employed by plantation owners in the Cotton Delta of eastern Arkansas arrived at John Handcox's ramshackle home, with guns in hand and trouble in mind. Handcox helped organize the Southern Tenant Farmers Union, which had pulled hundreds of sharecroppers and tenant farmers out on strike for better wages and working conditions. . . . But Handcox was not home that day. . . . "My grandfather was a slave . . . I'd ask him questions about slavery. . . . When I was a kid, I used to write poems, but when the union picked up, that's when I started on songs. . . . I tried to write something interesting about the conditions that people were living under and what was happening—pointing out to people when they were working hard and not getting anything out of it. . . ." *Roll the Union On* is one of the songs that John Handcox wrote in the 1930s for the Southern Tenant Farmers Union. It is a good example of a "zipper song"—you can add anybody's name and "roll right over him."

ROLL THE UNION ON

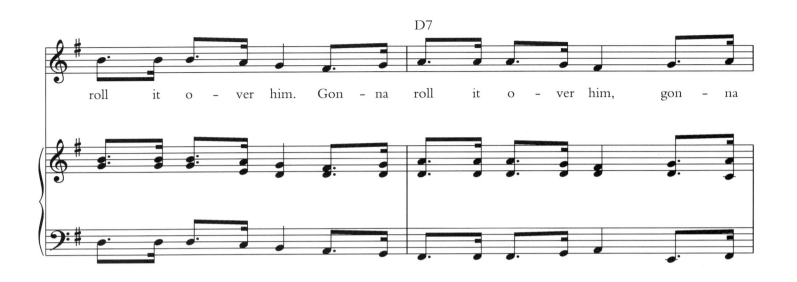

roll it o - ver him. Gon - na roll it o - ver him, gon - na

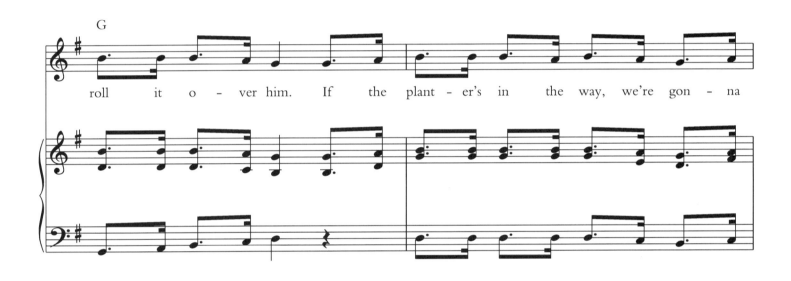

roll it o - ver him. If the plant - er's in the way, we're gon - na

roll it o - ver him. Gon - na roll _____ the un - ion on.

D. C.

If the boss is in the way, We're gonna roll it over over him. Gonna roll it over him, Gonna roll it over him. If the boss is in the way, We're gonna roll it over him. Gonna roll the union on. *Chorus*	If the merchant's in the way . . . *Chorus* If the banker's in the way . . . *Chorus* If the preacher's in the way . . . *Chorus* If Wall Street's in the way . . . *Chorus*

This fine old spiritual lends itself perfectly to present-day circumstances. It is another good example of the Promised Land motif.

I'M ON MY WAY
TO THE FREEDOM LAND

I'm on my way _____ to the free - dom land, _____

_____ I'm on my way _____ to the free - dom land, _____

_____ I'm on my way _____ to the free - dom land, _____

I'm on my way, Great God, I'm on my way.

I'll ask my brother to come and go with me, (3)
I'm on my way, Great God, I'm on my way.

If he can't go, I'm gonna go anyhow, (3)
I'm on my way, Great God, I'm on my way.

If you can't go, don't hinder me, (3)
I'm on my way, Great God, I'm on my way.

If you can't go, let your children go, (3)
I'm on my way, Great God, I'm on my way.

*On their way to freedom land, Dr. Martin Luther King, Jr., leads thousands of
followers on the Selma-to-Montgomery march in 1965.*

Index to titles

Index to first lines

Jerry Silverman is one of America's most prolific authors of music books. He has a B.S. degree in music from the City College of New York and an M.A. in musicology from New York University. He has authored some 100 books dealing with various aspects of guitar, banjo, violin, and fiddle technique, as well as numerous songbooks and arrangements for other instruments. He teaches guitar and music to children and adults and performs in folk-song concerts before audiences of all ages.

Kenneth B. Clark received a Ph.D. in social psychology from Columbia University and is the author of numerous books and articles on race and education. His books include *Prejudice and Your Child, Dark Ghetto,* and *Pathos of Power.* Long noted as an authority on segregation in schools, his work was cited by the U.S. Supreme Court in its decision in the historic case *Brown* v. *Board of Education of Topeka* case in 1954. Dr. Clark, Distinguished Professor of Psychology Emeritus at the City University of New York, is the president of Kenneth B. Clark & Associates, a consulting firm specializing in personnel matters, race relations, and affirmative action programs.